ABERCROMBIE & FITCH

Estab. 1892

Compiled by

MARY ALICE WARNER

Illustrated by

THOMAS SPERLING

A COLLECTION OF QUOTATIONS,

BOTH HUMOROUS AND SERIOUS, ABOUT

THE SWEET AND NOT-SO-SWEET SMELL

OF SUCCESS.

SPEAKING OF SUCCESS

The road to success is always under construction.

Sometimes I worry about being a success in a mediocre world.

LILY TOMLIN

I don't know the key to success, but the key to failure is trying to please everybody.

BILL COSBY

Success is getting what you want; happiness is wanting what you get.

Success comes in cans, failure in can'ts.

Success is the best perfume.

ELIZABETH TAYLOR

Becoming number one is easier than remaining number one .

BILL BRADLEY

Success is to be measured not so much by the position that one has reached in life as by the obstacles which one has overcome while trying to succeed.

BOOKER T. WASHINGTON

They say getting thin is the best revenge. Success is much better.

OPRAH WINFREY

As for the *act* of sex, I think passion for work and passion for a man are totally related—you do *everything* with energy and heat. So, yes: you can love deeply *and* be an enormous success.

HELEN GURLEY BROWN

Winning isn't everything. It's the only thing.
VINCE LOMBARDI

The dictionary is the only place where success comes before work.

ARTHUR BRISBANE

The secret of business is to know something that nobody else knows.

ARISTOTLE ONASSIS

The road to success is filled with women pushing their husbands along.

THOMAS R. DEWAR

In Hollywood success is relative. The closer the relative, the greater the success.

ARTHUR TREACHER

To be successful, a woman has to be much better at her job than a man.

GOLDA MEIR

If you fail, it's because you took a chance; if you succeed, it's because you grasped an opportunity.

He has achieved success who has lived well, laughed often and loved much.

BESSIE ANDERSON STANLEY

Your success and happiness lie in you.

HELEN KELLER

People seldom see the halting and painful steps by which the most insignificant success is achieved.

ANNIE SULLIVAN

Success depends on three things: who says it, what he says, how he says it; and of these three things, what he says is the least important.

JOHN, VISCOUNT MORLEY OF BLACKBURN

You can't climb the ladder of success with cold feet.

There may be splinters on the ladder of success, but you don't notice them until you slide down.

If at first you do succeed, don't take any more chances.

FRANK MCKINNEY HUBBARD

If at first you don't succeed, you'll probably have more friends.

There is an old motto that runs, "If at first you don't succeed, try, try again." This is nonsense. It ought to read, "If at first you don't succeed, quit, quit at once."

STEPHEN LEACOCK

Nothing succeeds like success.

ALEXANDRE DUMAS, PÈRE

Nothing succeeds like excess.

LIFE

A successful man is one who earns more than his wife can possibly spend. A successful woman is the wife who manages to spend it all the same.

SACHA GUITRY

Every man who is high up loves to think that he has done it all himself; and the wife smiles, and lets it go at that.

J. M. BARRIE

Many a man owes his success to his first wife and his second wife to his success.

RED BUTTONS

Success is like a liberation or the first phase of a love story.

JEANNE MOREAU

Happiness is not having what you want, but wanting what you have.

RABBI HYMAN JUDAH SCHACHTEL

Love can be had any day! Success is far harder.

ENID BAGNOLD

Success has ruin'd many a man.

BENJAMIN FRANKLIN

Nothing succeeds like success, except the failure that reverses it.

L. STEIN

Nothing recedes like success.

WALTER WINCHELL

On the door to success it says: push and pull.

YIDDISH PROVERB

The law of success: more bone in the back and less in the head.

Nature gave men two ends—one to sit on and one to think with. Ever since then man's success or failure has been dependent on the one he used most.

GEORGE R. KIRKPATRICK

When a man blames others for his failures, it's a good idea to credit others with his successes.

HOWARD W. NEWTON

She's the kind of girl who climbed the ladder of success, wrong by wrong.

MAE WEST

The successful person is the one who went ahead and did the thing I always intended to do.

RUTH SMELTZER

Success has the character of a cat. It won't come when coaxed.

FRANZ WERFEL

Try not to become a man of success but rather try to become a man of value.

ALBERT EINSTEIN

The secret really seems to be hard work, thorough preparation, detailed knowledge, careful planning, tight organization, strong leadership, dogged persistence, controlled energy, good instincts and the genetic ability to deal.

CHRISTOPHER LEHMANN-HAUPT,
on Donald J. Trump

The Talmud says there are three things one should do in the course of one's life: have a child, plant a tree, and write a book.

HAROLD KUSHNER

Success is that old ABC—ability, breaks and courage.

CHARLES LUCKMAN

If A equals success, then the formula is A equals X plus Y plus Z. X is work. Y is play. Z is keep your mouth shut.

ALBERT EINSTEIN

Greatness is so often a courteous synonym for great success.

GUEDALLA

To get it right, be born with luck or else make it. *Never* give up. Get the knack of getting people to help you and also pitch in yourself. A little money helps, but what *really* gets it right is to *never*—I repeat—*never,* under any condition face the facts.

RUTH GORDON

A touch of folly is needed if we are to extricate ourselves successfully from some of the hazards of life.

LA ROCHEFOUCAULD

To succeed in the world, we do everything we can to appear successful.

LA ROCHEFOUCAULD

Nothing is so impudent as Success—unless it be those she favours.

J. R. PLANCHÉ

To succeed in the other trades, capacity must be shown; in the law, concealment of it will do.

MARK TWAIN

All you need in this life is ignorance and confidence, and then success is sure.

MARK TWAIN

Success is the child of Audacity.

BENJAMIN DISRAELI

Part of the secret of success in life is to eat what you like and let the food fight it out inside.

MARK TWAIN

Let us be thankful for the fools. But for them the rest of us could not succeed.

MARK TWAIN

The worst use that can be made of success is to boast of it.

ARTHUR HELPS

The men who pass most comfortably through the world are those who possess good digestion and hard hearts.

HARRIET MARTINEAU

To know how to wait is the great secret of success.

DE MAISTRE

The gent who wakes up and finds himself a success hasn't been asleep.

WILSON MIZNER

Success may go to one's head but the stomach is where it gets in its worst work.

FRANK McKINNEY HUBBARD

He owed his success neither to distinguished abilities, nor to skill-supplying industry, but to the art of uniting suppleness to others with confidence in himself.

FRANCES BURNEY

Success in life means doing that thing than which nothing else conceivable seems more noble or satisfying or remunerative.

ALAN SEEGER

Success is something to enjoy—to flaunt! Otherwise, why work so hard to get it?

ISOBEL LENNART

From the Taoist point of view, an educated man is one who believes he has not succeeded when he has, but is not so sure he has failed when he fails.

LIN YUTANG

Success in life depends on two things: luck and pluck, luck in finding someone to pluck.

WYNN

In public we say the race is to the strongest; in private we know that a lopsided man runs the fastest along the little side-hills of success.

FRANK M. COLBY

The secret of success in life is known only to those who have not succeeded.

CHURTON COLLINS

If you wish to be a success in the world, acquire a knowledge of Latin, a horse, and money.

SPANISH PROVERB

People occasionally fall ill precisely because a deeply rooted and long cherished wish has come to fulfillment. It seems as though they could not endure their bliss.

SIGMUND FREUD

Life is a series of moments/to live each one is to succeed.

CORITA KENT

Love once—e'en love's disappointment
  endears!
A minute's success pays the failure of years.

ROBERT BROWNING

Toil, solitude, prayer.

NICCOLO PAGANINI, *when asked to give the secret of his success*

Everyone is a genius at least once a year. The real geniuses simply have their bright ideas closer together.

GEORGE C. LICHTENBERG

Success four flights Thursday morning all against twenty-one mile wind started from level with engine power alone average speed through air thirty-one miles longest 59 seconds inform press home Christmas.

ORVILLE AND WILBUR WRIGHT *(telegram to their father)*

Success can corrupt; usefulness can only exalt.

Dimitri Mitropolous

I have not failed. I have [successfully] discovered twelve hundred materials that won't work.

Thomas Edison

These three things, Work, Will, Success, fill human existence.

Louis Pasteur

A man who has been the indisputable favorite of his mother keeps for life the feeling of a conqueror, that confidence of success that often induces real success.

Sigmund Freud

There is nothing more difficult to take in hand, more perilous to conduct, or more uncertain in its success, than to take the lead in the introduction of a new order of things.

Nicolò Machiavelli

To play great music, you must keep your eyes on a distant star.

YEHUDI MENUHIN

If my success has been greater than that of most . . . the reason is that I came in my wanderings through the medical field upon regions where the gold was still lying by the wayside . . . and that is no great merit.

ROBERT KOCH

Be satisfied with success in even the smallest matter, and think that even such a result is no trifle.

MARCUS AURELIUS ANTONINUS

An earnest desire to succeed is almost always prognostic of success.

STANISLAUS LESZCYNSKI (KING OF POLAND)

To have any success in life, or any worthy success, you must resolve to carry into your work a fulness of knowledge—not merely a sufficiency, but more than a sufficiency.

JAMES A. GARFIELD

The secret of success is constancy to purpose.
BENJAMIN DISRAELI

Didst thou never hear
That things ill-got had ever bad success?
WILLIAM SHAKESPEARE
(Henry VI)

Always bear in mind that your own resolution
to succeed is more important than any other
one thing.

ABRAHAM LINCOLN

Young man, the secret of my success is that at
an early age I discovered I was not God.
OLIVER WENDELL HOLMES

The most important single ingredient in the
formula of success is knowing how to get
along with people.

THEODORE ROOSEVELT

Real success consists in doing one's duty well
in the path where one's life is led.
THEODORE ROOSEVELT

You seem to have no real purpose in life and won't realize at the age of twenty-two that for a man life means work, and hard work if you mean to succeed . . .

JENNIE JEROME CHURCHILL,
letter to Winston Churchill

The way to success in this great country, with its fair judgments, is to show that you are not afraid of anybody except God and His final verdict. If I did not believe that, I would not believe in democracy.

WOODROW WILSON

Most people are fascinated by outward success . . . If their external image is, for any reason, shaken, they are inevitably shaken and may even collapse.

ANWAR SADAT

One of the things Cell 54 taught me was to value that inner success which alone maintains one's inward equilibrium and helps a man to be true to himself. No man can be honest with others unless he is true to himself.

ANWAR SADAT

Outward success alienates a man from himself.
ANWAR SADAT

Success can make you go one of two ways. It can make you a prima donna, or it can smooth the edges, take away the insecurities, let the nice things come out.
BARBARA WALTERS

To feel valued, to know, even if only once in a while, that you can do a job well is an absolutely marvelous feeling.
BARBARA WALTERS

The best part of one's life is the working part, the creative part. Believe me, I love to succeed ... However, the real spiritual and emotional excitement is in the doing.
GARSON KANIN

I've never sought success in order to get fame and money; it's the talent and the passion that count in success.
INGRID BERGMAN

Any man who has come up through the process of political selection ... knows that success is a mixture of principles steadfastly maintained and adjustments made at the proper time and place—adjustments to conditions, not adjustment of principles.

HARRY S TRUMAN

Success is not a harbor but a voyage with its own perils to the spirit. The game of life is to come up a winner, to be a success, or to achieve what we set out to do. Yet there is always the danger of failing as a human being. The lesson that most of us on this voyage never learn, but can never quite forget, is that to win is sometimes to lose.

RICHARD M. NIXON

I have the best of both worlds. A Harvard education and a Yale degree.

JOHN F. KENNEDY

One's religion is whatever he is most interested in, and yours is Success.

JAMES M. BARRIE

Nothing in the world can take the place of persistence. Talent will not; nothing is more common than unsuccessful men with talent. Genius will not; unrewarded genius is almost a proverb. Education will not; the world is full of educated derelicts. Persistence and determination alone are omnipotent!

CALVIN COOLIDGE

To stand upon the ramparts and die for our principles is heroic, but to sally forth to battle and win for our principles is something more than heroic.

FRANKLIN D. ROOSEVELT

A formula for success: first and foremost, being funny.

DON RICKLES

Success, which touches nothing that it does not vulgarize, should be its own reward . . . the odium of success is hard enough to bear, without the added ignominy of popular applause.

ROBERT BONTINE CUNNINGHAME GRAHAM

Can success change the human mechanism so completely between one dawn and another? Can it make one feel taller, more alive, handsomer, uncommonly gifted and indomitably secure with the certainty that this is the way life will always be? It can and it does!

MOSS HART

To tend, unfailingly, unflinchingly, towards a goal, is the secret of success. But success? What exactly is success? For me it is to be found . . . in the satisfaction of feeling that one is realising one's ideal.

ANNA PAVLOVA

My aim was never liberation—it was survival. I simply say to women, "Be liberated if you wish—but be *successful.*"

TINA TURNER

For an actress to be a success she must have the face of Venus, the brains of Minerva, the grace of Terpsichore, the memory of Macaulay, the figure of Juno, and the hide of a rhinoceros.

ETHEL BARRYMORE

The toughest thing about success is that you've got to keep on being a success.

IRVING BERLIN

Success is important only to the extent that it puts one in a position to do more things one likes to do.

SARAH CALDWELL

Success to me is having ten honeydew melons and eating only the top half of each one.

BARBRA STREISAND

. . . it is a peaceful thing to be one succeeding.

GERTRUDE STEIN

Life lives only in success.

BAYARD TAYLOR

It is very easy to succeed in spite of poverty. It is difficult to succeed in spite of wealth.

ARTHUR BRISBANE

All my life I've always had the urge to do things better than anybody else. Even in school . . . I'd want mine to be the best in the class.

BABE DIDRIKSON ZAHARIAS

Basketball can serve as a kind of metaphor for ultimate cooperation. It is a sport where success, as symbolized by the championship, requires that the dictates of community prevail over selfish personal impulses.

BILL BRADLEY

Believe in yourself! Have faith in your abilities! Without a humble but reasonable confidence in your own powers you cannot be successful or happy.

NORMAN VINCENT PEALE

The heights by great men reached and kept,
Were not attained by sudden flight—
But they, while their companions slept,
Were toiling upward in the night.

HENRY WADSWORTH LONGFELLOW

The great majority of conspicuously successful men are early risers.... Moral: To get up in the world, get up early in the morning.

B. C. FORBES

There's one meaningful definition of success—doing what turns you on, doing what you most want to be doing.

MALCOLM FORBES

The fastest way to succeed is to look as if you're playing by other people's rules, while quietly playing by your own.

MICHAEL KORDA

Every man should make up his mind that if he expects to succeed, he must give an honest return for the other man's dollar.

EDWARD H. HARRIMAN

If you want to know whether you are destined to be a success or a failure in life ... the test is simple and it is infallible. Are you able to save money? If not, drop out. You will lose.

JAMES J. HILL

Five things are essential to success: one is wealth, and the other four are money.

The typical successful American businessman was born in the country, where he worked like hell so he could live in the city, where he worked like hell so he could live in the country.

DON MARQUIS

I was able to focus in on intimidation as the key to winning.

ROBERT J. RINGER

The only successful substitute for brains is silence.

HERBERT V. PROCHNOW

Successfully to accomplish any task it is necessary not only that you should give it the best there is in you, but that you should obtain for it the best there is in those under your guidance.

GEORGE W. GOETHALS

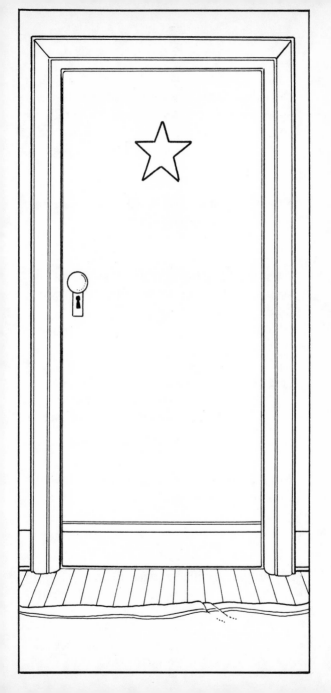

The best way to get on in the world is to make people believe it's to their advantage to help you.

JEAN DE LA BRUYÈRE

The victory of success is half won when one gains the habit of work.

What though success will not attend on all, Who bravely dares must sometimes risk a fall.

SMOLLETT

I git thar fustest with the mostest men.

NATHAN BEDFORD FORREST,
giving his formula for military success

We can't all be heroes. Somebody has to sit on the curb and clap as they go by.

WILL ROGERS

Sweat plus sacrifice equals success.

CHARLES O. FINLEY

It is never a sign of weakness when a man in high position delegates authority; on the contrary, it is a sign of his strength and of his capacity to deserve success.

WALTER LIPPMANN

The secret of success lies not in doing your own work, but in recognizing the right man to do it.

ANDREW CARNEGIE

In many businesses, today will end at five o'clock. Those bent on success, however, make today last from yesterday right through tomorrow.

LAWRENCE H. MARTIN

Success in life often consists in knowing just when to disagree with one's employer.

Nothing splendid has ever been achieved except by those who dared believe that something inside them was superior to circumstance.

BRUCE BARTON

Don't try to be the richest man in the world, for you will always have Rockefellers and Morgans. Don't try to be the strongest man in the world, for there will always be someone stronger. But have five minutes more patience than your opponent, and you will be the victor.

NICOLAS RISINI

The man who starts out with the idea of getting rich won't succeed: you must have a larger ambition. There is no mystery in business success. If you do each day's task successfully, stay faithful within the natural operations of commercial law, and keep your head clear, you will come out all right.

JOHN D. ROCKEFELLER

If you have a lemon, make lemonade.

HOWARD GOSSAGE

The broader definition of success I am searching for will neither consign women to the home and dependence on men nor nail them to a cross of professionalism.

HILARY COSELL

There are two ways of rising in the world: either by one's own industry or profiting by the foolishness of others.

LA BRUYÈRE

True success is achieved when you have made the best use of your time for a worthy purpose, when you have ... developed your physical and mental equipment to the highest possible degree of efficiency. Health, contentment and happiness are the rewards of the right use of your equipment.

DR. HAMILTON CAMERON

If at first you don't succeed you're running about average.

M. H. ALDERSON

Old age is like everything else. To make a success of it, you've got to start young.

FRED ASTAIRE

We might all be successful if we followed the advice we give the other fellow.

It is doubtful if anyone ever made a success of anything who waited until all the conditions were "just right" before starting.

Success is not rare—it is common ... It is a matter of adjusting one's efforts to obstacles and one's abilities to a service needed by others. There is no other possible success. But most people think of it in terms of getting; success, however, begins in terms of giving.

HENRY FORD, SR.

Successful salesman: someone who has found a cure for the common cold shoulder.

ROBERT ORBEN

America celebrates success, but occasionally it pauses to regret the men who didn't quite make it.

JAMES RESTON

Success—"the bitch-goddess, Success," in William James's phrase—demands strange sacrifices from those who worship her.

ALDOUS HUXLEY

You have reached the pinnacle of success as soon as you become uninterested in money, compliments, or publicity.

DR. O. A. BATTISTA

The secret of success is not to mope, and to get out of bed in the morning.

MALCOLM COWLEY

Success means never having to admit you're unhappy.

ROBERT EVANS

The whole art of practical success consists in concentrating all efforts at all times upon one point.

LASSALLE

Real success is not an outward show but an inward feeling . . . that one is worth while. That's quite a discovery. Regardless of how the rest of the world may value us, there is no fooling the inner Bureau of Standards.

HOWARD J. WHITMAN

One of the biggest troubles with success these days is that its recipe is about the same as that for a nervous breakdown.

Success begins with a fellow's will—it's all in the state of mind.

WALTER D. WINTLE

True success is overcoming the fear of being unsuccessful.

PAUL SEENEY

The sort of success I mean consists of this: getting to do what you really want to do in your work life and in your love life, doing it very well, and feeling good about yourself doing it. The fear of success is not getting what you really want because you unconsciously feel you don't deserve it.

MARTHA FRIEDMAN

The penalty of success is to be bored by the attentions of people who formerly snubbed you.

MARY WILSON LITTLE

The best thing that can come with success is the knowledge that it is nothing to long for.

LIV ULLMANN

They [girls] were not simply eager to fail and have done with it, they seemed to be in a state of anxious conflict over what would happen if they succeeded. It was almost as though this conflict was inhibiting their capacity for achievement.

MATINA HORNER

It is more complicated and expensive to look like a successful woman than it is a successful man, particularly in a man's world.

JOHN T. MOLLOY

Nothing succeeds like looking successful.

HENRIETTE CORKLAND

Traditionally, women have had trouble claiming their successes as the direct result of their own abilities.

GAIL SHEEHY

There would be more incentive to success if successful men seemed to enjoy life more.

Women . . . are almost never heroes . . . [but] women who *have* had any success find that in fact, it is more pleasant than failing.

CYNTHIA FUCHS EPSTEIN

Failure is often that early morning hour of darkness which precedes the dawning of the day of success.

LEIGH MITCHELL HODGES

The idea has gained currency that women have often been handicapped not only by a fear of failure—not unknown to men either— but by a fear of success as well.

SONYA RUDIKOFF

The dilemma then is how women can "make it in a man's world" but reject, as a condition for that success, becoming part of the machinery that keeps this a man's world.

PHYLLIS CHESLER

The most successful negotiators are those who continue to find mutual rewards and who ask for cooperation despite the reluctance of people who are still making up their minds.

JARD DEVILLE

A financially rewarding career reflects mental health and not mere wanton pursuit of the Bitch Goddess Success.

GEORGE VAILLANT

The moral flabbiness born of the exclusive worship of the bitch-goddess SUCCESS. That—with the squalid cash interpretation put on the word success—is our national disease.

WILLIAM JAMES

Like William James, he [Henry George] saw success as a bitch-goddess and simply did not like her company.

GERALD W. JOHNSON

Personal success often involves a great social consciousness as well.

GEORGE GALLUP, JR., AND ALEC M. GALLUP

Blue collar women like myself have limited opportunities for success on the job. Our only chance to excel is in the union movement or at home.

DOROTHY HAENER

Being black and female starts one off very low on the success ladder . . . Trust your judgment and take risks. Believe in yourself. You have to be shrewd to survive on the marketplace.

NAOMI SIMS

There is no *way* to succeed and have the lovely spoils—money, recognition, *deep* satisfaction in your work—except to put in the hours, do the drudgery . . . Nearly every glamorous, wealthy, successful career woman you might envy *now* started as some kind of shlep.

HELEN GURLEY BROWN

We learn wisdom from failure much more than from success. We often discover what *will* do, by finding out what will not do; and probably he who never made a mistake never made a discovery.

SAMUEL SMILES

Success is when you're personally satisfied with what you've accomplished. Fame is when others see you as successful for reasons that may or may not meet your standards.

BELLA S. ABZUG

The mother is the one supreme asset of national life; she is more important by far than the successful statesman, or businessman, or artist, or scientist.

THEODORE ROOSEVELT

Women share with men the need for personal success, even the taste for power, and no longer are we willing to satisfy those needs through the achievements of surrogates, whether husbands, children or merely role models.

ELIZABETH DOLE

The highest pinnacle of success in life is achieved by consecration of one's self to an ideal and the readiness to make sacrifices for it.

ETHEL JUDENSEN

I've always believed that one woman's success can only help another woman's success.

GLORIA VANDERBILT

Success in men's eyes is God and more than God.

AESCHYLUS

Success, remember, is the reward of toil.

SOPHOCLES

Along with success comes a reputation for wisdom.

EURIPIDES

It is not the going out of port, but the coming in, that determines the success of a voyage.

H. W. BEECHER

If one advances confidently in the direction of his dreams, and endeavors to live the life which he has imagined, he will meet with a success unexpected in common hours.

HENRY D. THOREAU

47

The common idea that success spoils people by making them vain, egotistic, and self-complacent is erroneous; on the contrary, it makes them, for the most part, humble, tolerant, and kind.

SOMERSET MAUGHAM

I have always observed that to succeed in the world one should seem a fool, but be wise.

MONTESQUIEU

If Fortune wishes to make a man estimable, she gives him virtue; if she wishes to make him esteemed, she gives him success.

JOUBERT

All succeeds with people who are sweet and cheerful.

VOLTAIRE

A man may be festooned with the whole haberdashery of success, and go to his grave a castaway.

RUDYARD KIPLING

'Tis man's to fight, but Heaven's to give success.

HOMER

Success is a rare paint, hides all the ugliness.

SIR JOHN SUCKLING

We never know, believe me, when we have succeeded best.

UNAMUNO

When people call me a success, I feel falsely accused. I might feel successful if I could write one book that mattered.

GLORIA STEINEM

Success is counted sweetest
By those who ne'er succeed.

EMILY DICKINSON

In all things, success depends upon previous preparation, and without such preparation there is sure to be failure.

CONFUCIUS

If a man has a talent and cannot use it, he has failed. If he has a talent and uses only half of it, he has partly failed. If he has a talent and learns somehow to use the whole of it, he has gloriously succeeded, and won a satisfaction and a triumph few men ever know.

THOMAS WOLFE

One significant activity that distinguishes high achievers from their less successful counterparts is their love of reading—and their corresponding lack of interest in television.

GEORGE GALLUP, JR., AND ALEC M. GALLUP

Men die; devices change; success and fame run their course. But within the walls of even the smallest library in our land lie the treasures, the wisdom and the wonder of man's greatest adventures on this earth.

LEO ROSTEN

The talent of success is nothing more than doing what you can do well; and doing well whatever you do, without a thought of fame.

HENRY WADSWORTH LONGFELLOW

So in each action 'tis success
That gives it all its comeliness.

WILLIAM SOMERVILLE

Success, as I see it, is a result, not a goal.

GUSTAVE FLAUBERT

Our business in this world is not to succeed,
but to continue to fail, in good spirits.

ROBERT LOUIS STEVENSON

Failure is very difficult for a writer to bear, but
very few can manage the shock of early
success.

MAURICE VALENCY

One can live magnificently in this world, if
one knows how to work and how to love, to
work for the person one loves and to love
one's work.

LEO TOLSTOY

Success is no proof of virtue.

WALTER KAUFMANN

I dread success. To have succeeded is to have finished one's business on earth, like the male spider, who is killed by the female the moment he has succeeded in his courtship. I like a state of continual becoming, with a goal in front and not behind.

GEORGE BERNARD SHAW

Well, if I don't succeed, I have succeeded, And that's enough.

BYRON

Success in almost any field depends more on energy and drive than it does on intelligence. This explains why we have so many stupid leaders.

SLOAN WILSON

Success is the necessary misfortune of life, but it is only to the very unfortunate that it comes early.

ANTHONY TROLLOPE

Self-trust is the first secret of success.

RALPH WALDO EMERSON

If a man loves the labor of his trade, apart from any question of success or fame, the gods have called him.

ROBERT LOUIS STEVENSON

Everything bows to success, even grammar.

VICTOR HUGO

Really the writer doesn't want success . . . He knows he has a short span of life, that the day will come when he must pass through the wall of oblivion, and he wants to leave a scratch on that wall—Kilroy was here—that somebody a hundred, or a thousand years later will see.

WILLIAM FAULKNER

The surest way not to fail is to determine to succeed.

SHERIDAN

Often a certain abdication of prudence and foresight is an element of success.

RALPH WALDO EMERSON

In order that people may be happy in their work, these three things are needed: They must be fit for it. They must not do too much of it. And they must have a sense of success in it.

JOHN RUSKIN

The success of any great moral enterprise does not depend upon numbers.

WILLIAM LLOYD GARRISON

Anybody can sympathize with the sufferings of a friend, but it requires a very fine nature to sympathize with a friend's success.

OSCAR WILDE

We get very little wisdom from success, you know. Success makes a fool of you, but failure can come only from great effort. One who doesn't try cannot fail and become wise.

WILLIAM SAROYAN

[Success is getting] people to do what you want and thank you for it.

JARD DeVILLE

What is known as success assumes nearly as many aliases as there are those who seek it. Like love, it can come to commoners as well as courtiers. Like virtue, it is its own reward. Like the Holy Grail, it seldom appears to those who don't pursue it.

STEPHEN BIRMINGHAM

Success isn't everything but it makes a man stand straight.

LILLIAN HELLMAN

In this world there are only two tragedies. One is not getting what one wants, and the other is getting it.

OSCAR WILDE

The great secret of a successful honeymoon is to treat all disasters as incidents and none of the incidents as disasters.

HAROLD NICHOLSON

The success of the marriage comes after the failure of the honeymoon.

G. K. CHESTERTON

Success is a fickle jade. The clothes on her back may be put there by hard work, but her jewels are the gifts of chance.

SIR CHARLES WHEELER

The compensation of very early success is a conviction that life is a romantic matter. In the best sense one stays young.

F. SCOTT FITZGERALD

There is a vast difference between success at twenty-five and success at sixty. At sixty, nobody envies you. Instead, everybody rejoices generously, sincerely, in your good fortune.

MARIE DRESSLER

In the aging game success is dependent on a calculated program of resistance to society's planned disengagement of its old.

BARBARA GALLATIN ANDERSON

How can they say my life isn't a success? Have I not for more than sixty years got enough to eat and escaped being eaten?

LOGAN PEARSALL SMITH

I think success has no rules, but you can learn a great deal from failure.

JEAN KERR

The successful revolutionary is a statesman, the unsuccessful one a criminal.

ERICH FROMM

Happiness (joy) is proof of partial or total success in the "art of living."

ERICH FROMM

Health is not fame, nor fame health. Health is success at living.

GEORGE VAILLANT

The person who has discovered the pleasures of truly human living, the person whose life is rich in friendships and caring people, the person who enjoys daily the pleasures of good food and sunshine, will not need to wear herself out in pursuit of some other kind of success.

HAROLD KUSHNER

What gratifies me most about the success of my previous book is . . . having eight or ten people come up to me afterward to tell me, "Your book changed my life. I could never have made it through this past year without it."

HAROLD KUSHNER

Have little care that life is brief,
And less that art is long.
Success is in the silences
Though fame is in the song.

BLISS CARMAN

It takes twenty years to make an overnight success.

EDDIE CANTOR *(ATTRIBUTED)*

Success is energy.

FAYE DUNAWAY

The only good judge of success is me. The judgment of other people gives you a bit of confidence, but it's not everything.

ALESSANDRA FERRI

The only way to succeed is to make people hate you.

JOSEF VON STERNBERG

Every time a friend succeeds, I die a little.

GORE VIDAL

When men drink, then they are rich and successful and win lawsuits and are happy and help their friends.

ARISTOPHANES

There is no deodorant like success.

ELIZABETH TAYLOR

If you are mediocre and you grovel, you shall succeed.

PIERRE DE BEAUMARCHAIS

There is only one success—to be able to spend your life in your own way.

CHRISTOPHER MORLEY

First, I believe to be successful you must love your work and be dedicated to it. You must also have strong ties with your family and friends. And, you can't be successful in these goals unless you organize every hour of your day.

JEHAN SADAT

Aggressive, competitive behavior will not ensure success in the workplace or home.

SRULLY BLOTNICK

New things succeed, as former things grow old.

ROBERT HERRICK

If you don't watch out, success could kill you.

KENNETH BLANCHARD

You will be in a great position to have health and success if your relationship with God your Source is right.

ORAL ROBERTS

[Success is] doing what you love and having a positive impact on people's lives without starving to death.

GLORIA STEINEM

Success in the Personal Zone is a give-and-take affair between two equals. It is two unique human beings being together.

RICHARD CORRIERE AND
PATRICK M. McGRADY, JR.

With the help of other women I have finally come to understand my own definition of success: Love. Work. Knowledge. And not having to choose between them.

LETTY COTTIN POGREBIN

Fortune may have yet a better success in reserve for you, and they who lose to-day may win to-morrow.

MIGUEL DE CERVANTES

One thing is forever good;
That one thing is Success.
RALPH WALDO EMERSON

Next to Death, the most infallible remedy for a
guilty conscience is success.

Nothing succeeds like success, and nothing
fails like reading a book on how to attain it.